LEFT WITH NOTHING, BUILT EVERYTHING

HOW LOSING EVERYTHING PUSHED ME TO SUCCEED

Lema Fombin

Dedication

This book is dedicated to the broken, the betrayed, and the dreamers who still dare to rise. To the man or woman who feels invisible right now, holding the shattered pieces of a life they thought would last, I see you, because once I stood at the same place. And I wrote this book for you.

To the single parent fighting to keep hope alive. To the dreamer who has been told "no" one too many times. To the worker who gave everything to a job that discarded them without a second thought. To the spouse who loved deeply but was left behind. To the friend who wonders if tomorrow will look any different than today.

You are not forgotten. Your pain is not pointless. Your story is not finished.

And finally, I dedicate this book to the man I became in the ashes of loss, the man who chose to rise instead of surrender. Thank you for not quitting when it would have been easier to let go.

Acknowledgment

Writing this book has been both an act of healing and an act of faith. It would not have been possible without the grace of God, whose hand sustained me in the darkest valleys and whose light guided me toward new beginnings. To Him, I give the highest thanks, for carrying me when I could not stand, for whispering truth when lies screamed loudest, and for reminding me that storms never have the final word.

To my family and true friends, those who did not abandon me when I had nothing left to give, your loyalty was a lifeline. Thank you for being a reminder that genuine love is not conditional and that real relationships are not based on convenience.

To the mentors, coaches, and authors whose words found me in the midnight hours, thank you for being proof that resilience is possible. You reminded me that my pain was not unique, but my response to it could be.

To the readers of this book, whether you are picking it up from a bookstore shelf, an online shop, or receiving it as a gift from a friend: thank you. You are the reason I turned my wounds into words. If even one sentence in these pages reignites your hope, then every tear I shed was worth it.

And finally, to the pain itself, the betrayal, the heartbreak, the silence, the nights I thought I would not survive: thank you for becoming my greatest teacher. You stripped me bare so I could finally meet the man I was meant to become.

About the Author

LEMA FOMBIN is a storyteller, entrepreneur, and voice of resilience whose life journey embodies the very themes that echo through his book *Left With Nothing, Built Everything: How Losing Everything Pushed Me to Succeed.* His story is not one of unbroken triumph, but of rising again and again from the ashes of betrayal, financial loss, heartbreak, and shattered dreams.

He once built what appeared to be a perfect life: career stability, financial comfort, and the promise of lasting love, only to watch it all collapse. A sudden job loss stripped away his livelihood, a painful betrayal dismantled his marriage, and financial ruin left him staring at rock bottom with no safety net.

Yet, from that lowest point, Lema discovered a powerful truth: when you are left with nothing, you are finally free to rebuild everything. His journey of rebuilding was neither glamorous nor easy. It began on the floor of a nearly empty apartment, where the silence of heartbreak became the classroom for resilience. Through small steps, relentless hustle, new skills, and unshakable faith, he transformed pain into purpose and despair into determination.

His life is a living testimony that **failure is never final if you refuse to quit.**

As an author, Lema writes with raw honesty and emotional depth. He shares not only his scars but also the lessons those scars carry: that resilience is forged in silence, that betrayal can awaken hidden strength, and that true success is measured not by wealth or status but by peace, purpose, and impact. His writing merges memoir with empowerment, offering readers a mirror through which they can see their own strength reflected.

Beyond writing, Lema is dedicated to empowering others to rise from their own valleys of loss and betrayal. He speaks passionately about faith, perseverance, and the immigrant journey, bridging his African heritage with his global perspective. He believes in building legacies that outlive personal pain, legacies rooted in integrity, compassion, and courage.

Through his books and mentorship, Lema Fombin reminds the world that every setback carries within it the seed of a comeback. His mission is not simply to tell his story, but to ignite others to rewrite theirs.

Left With Nothing, Built Everything is more than a book; it is the anthem of his life, a beacon for those standing in ruins, and a declaration that the human spirit, though tested by betrayal and brokenness, can rise stronger, wiser, and unshakable.

Preface

When I first sat down to write, I was hesitant. Who would want to read about pain? Who would care about betrayal, heartbreak, and nights of despair? But as I reflected, I realized something powerful: pain unspoken becomes poison, but pain shared can become medicine.

This book is not simply a retelling of events. It is an invitation. An invitation to look at your own struggles differently. To see beyond the surface of suffering and discover the hidden strength beneath it.

I want to be clear: this is not a "how-to" manual with easy steps. Life doesn't work that way. What I offer here is authenticity. The raw truth of falling apart. The unfiltered lessons of rebuilding. The scars and the victories. The tears and the triumphs.

My hope is that by reading my story, you will see reflections of your own. And in those reflections, you will discover the courage to keep moving forward, even when the path is unclear.

I wrote this book to honor the silent fighters, those who remain standing even when life has knocked them flat. I wrote it because sometimes, all we need to begin again is proof that someone else did.

If I could rebuild my life from the ashes of betrayal, loss, and nothingness, then so can you. And this book is my way of walking with you as you do.

Introduction

Life is rarely lived in a straight line. Yet, most of us expect progress to look like a ladder: step by step, upward, predictable. But reality is different. Life is messy. It rises and falls, often without warning. One moment, you are celebrating achievements, building dreams, and living in love. Next, you are standing in the ruins of what once felt unshakable, wondering how it all fell apart so quickly.

This book was born out of that very tension, the space between who I thought I was and who life forced me to become. I didn't sit down to write this because my story is perfect. I wrote it because my story is painfully human.

I lost a career I believed was secure. I watched a marriage dissolve into betrayal. I discovered financial deceptions that left me reeling. And for a long time, I sat with the haunting belief that maybe I wasn't enough.

But here's the truth: the end of what you thought was your life can be the beginning of the life you were created to live. Pain, betrayal, heartbreak, and failure are not life's final words. They are catalysts. They are chisels that carve away what is false to reveal the core of who you truly are.

As you walk with me through these pages, you will not just see my descent into loss, but my climb back into purpose. You'll read about nights filled with silence and despair, but also about mornings where faith whispered, *"Get up and try again."* This book is for those who feel broken, abandoned, or left with nothing. It's a roadmap, not just of survival, but of resurrection.

My hope is that when you finish this journey with me, you won't simply applaud the comeback of one man. Instead, you'll feel the stirrings of your own.

Table of Contents

Chapter 1:
The Perfect Life (or So I Thought)

There was a time when my mornings began with a fresh cup of coffee and a heart full of pride. I was the man who rose early, suited up, and walked into my job with purpose. I had worked hard to earn my position and fought tooth and nail to climb from humble beginnings to the corner office. I wasn't born into wealth. Every inch of my life had been earned; one sacrifice, one all-nighter, one risk at a time.

And it all seemed worth it.

I lived in a nice home, drove a decent car, and was married to the woman I thought was the love of my life. She was beautiful, educated, well-spoken, everything a man could ask for. When we first met, I thought I had found my partner, my confidant, my forever. We laughed easily, traveled often, and made plans for a glowing future. At least, I did.

It's funny how love can blind you to the cracks in the glass. I was so focused on building a kingdom for us that I never noticed she wasn't really helping lay the bricks. She enjoyed the comfort, yes. The lifestyle, the benefits, but the commitment? The sacrifice? The loyalty? Those were one-sided.

Still, I didn't see it.

Why would I? We had date nights, took selfies at airports; she smiled in pictures, and I mistook all of that for fulfillment, never realizing I was the only one still invested in our future.

But life has a brutal way of revealing truth, not through chaos, but through the quiet.

It started small; she stopped asking how my day was, then she stopped waiting for me to get home before eating dinner. Slowly, she became a roommate instead of a partner. Her eyes didn't light up when she saw me anymore, and our conversations became short. Her phone was always face down, and excuses became frequent, but I refused to believe anything was wrong.

I thought she was just stressed, but I convinced myself it was a phase. All couples go through dry spells, and since I was a man who prided himself on fixing problems, I did what I always did: I worked harder.

I worked longer, earned more, thinking money would fix what attention and intimacy no longer could.

I see now how deeply I misunderstood love. I thought love was something you earned. Something you worked for and proved, over and over. But real love doesn't need convincing; it stands beside you when the storm comes, and it holds your hand when you're drowning, not just when you're flying.

But she didn't sign up for the storm; she only wanted the sunshine.

And life was about to change, fast.

What makes this part of the story so painful isn't just the betrayal I would later discover. It's the realization that I had spent years building a life with someone who never truly saw me. I had invested my heart, my time, my soul into an illusion.

Yet, as strange as it sounds, I thank God for it now.

Because if I had continued living that perfect lie, I never would've discovered the strength hiding beneath my heartbreak. I never would've known the power of standing alone. I never would've been forced to dig deeper, climb higher, and fight harder, not for her, but for **me**.

Pain, as I've come to learn, is the universe's way of planting purpose.

You may be reading this today feeling broken, abandoned, or defeated. Maybe someone you trusted walked away when you needed them most, or perhaps life threw you off the path you planned, and you're staring at the pieces, wondering how you'll ever feel whole again.

Let me tell you this: **you're not at the end. You're at the beginning.**

Because I thought I had it all, then I lost everything, and that loss was the greatest gift of my life.

That season of false peace, of silent betrayal, and misplaced loyalty, it burned me down to nothing. But it also cleared the ground for the man I was meant to become.

This chapter, while painful, is sacred. Because it was the moment I realized something vital:

Comfort can be the enemy of growth. And betrayal can be the spark that ignites transformation.

The life I thought was perfect? It was just the shell. What lay beneath, the brokenness, the truth, the pain, that's where the real gold was buried.

If you're in a similar place, holding onto someone or something that's slipping away... let go, not out of anger, but out of faith. Because when life strips you bare, it's not trying to destroy you, it's trying to rebuild you.

The man I became started the moment I was left with nothing.

And from that emptiness, I built **everything**.

Chapter 2:
The Sudden Storm

The worst storms in life often come without warning, no forecast, no time to prepare; clouds that gather silently, then unleash all at once.

That's exactly how it happened.

One morning, I woke up to the usual sound of my alarm, stretched my arms, and followed my normal routine: shower, coffee, suit, quick kiss on her cheek, and then out the door. I had no idea that by noon, everything I knew would be ripped away from me.

I remember the email.

Subject: **Mandatory Department Meeting**

Time: **11:30 a.m.**

Location: **Conference Room A**

I didn't think much of it. Meetings came and went all the time. I assumed it was some organizational update, maybe another client win, maybe another motivational speech from leadership.

Instead, it was a corporate execution. Thirty-five of us were called into that room. One by one, we were handed envelopes, told it was "nothing personal," and just like that, jobs, careers, stability, gone.

My heart pounded, and I could barely process the words coming out of the HR manager's mouth. My hands trembled as I opened the envelope. Inside was a severance package and a checklist of items to return: laptop, company badge, and parking pass.

It felt like I had been punched in the chest.

I had given that company years of loyalty. I had missed birthdays, anniversaries, and moments that mattered, all in the name of "grinding" and "proving myself." I thought I was building something. I thought I was indispensable.

But in the blink of an eye, I became just another name on a list.

And still, I thought, *at least I have her.*

That was my first thought. That even though I lost my job, I had a partner at home who would understand. Who would lift me when I fell? Who would remind me of my worth?

But when I walked through that door with my box of belongings and broken pride, I was met with silence.

No hug nor any words of encouragement. Just a cold glance, a brief nod, and then she turned her attention back to her phone like nothing had happened.

"Wow," she finally said after a few minutes. "So, what's the plan now?"

The plan? I had just lost everything, and all she cared about was the plan?

That night, I sat on the couch long after she went to bed. I stared at the ceiling, trying to hold back tears. Not because of the job, but because I could feel her slipping away. Her warmth, her affection, her loyalty, it was already gone.

Losing the job wasn't the storm.

It was just the lightning strike that illuminated what had already been brewing in the dark for months.

I started noticing how distant she had become. The late nights at "work," the locked phone, the sudden need for "me time," the irritation in her voice when I spoke, it wasn't just stress, it wasn't just worry; instead, it was detachment. Emotional departure.

She had left, emotionally, long before she ever walked out the door.

But I was still fighting for us, still convincing myself that once I get another job, things will go back to normal. That maybe, just maybe, we were going through a rough patch.

But you can't fix something alone that was never held together by both hands.

I applied to dozens of jobs the following week. I polished my résumé, sent cold emails, and networked with old contacts. Every day,

I woke up determined to get back on my feet. I refused to stay down. I was willing to do anything to restore what I lost.

But she didn't see that, or maybe she didn't care to. Her words grew fewer, her sighs louder, her patience thinner.

One night, I overheard her on the phone with a friend; she didn't know I was awake.

"I can't do this anymore. He's not the man I married," she said.

And that hit me like a train.

Not the man she married? Because I was struggling? Because I was human?

What happened to *for better or worse*?

What happened to *in sickness or health*?

What happened to *I got you*?

Let me tell you something: **a storm doesn't destroy you, it reveals who's willing to shelter with you.**

I wasn't angry yet, not then. I was still holding on to hope and still believing that love would pull us through. That once I got back up, we'd look back on this moment and say, "We survived it."

But storms have a way of showing you who belongs in your life, and who was only there for the sunshine.

And this storm? It showed me everything I needed to see.

It showed me that I was more alone than I ever realized.

It showed me that people can promise forever and still walk away.

It showed me that when everything you leaned on collapses, you have only two choices: **break down, or break through.**

I wasn't ready to break through yet, but the decision was brewing, and the fight was stirring inside me.

Because deep down, I knew:

This storm wasn't the end of my story, and it was the wind I needed to rise.

Chapter 3:
The Cold Silence

Silence can be louder than screams.

After the layoff, the energy in our home shifted, and not in a subtle way. It wasn't just the absence of money or the stress of uncertainty. It was something deeper, something more painful. It was the quiet retreat of someone who had already emotionally checked out but didn't have the courage to walk away.

I still remember waking up early each morning, jobless but determined, wearing that same wrinkled button-down shirt as I sat in front of my laptop applying to every opportunity I could find. I'd rehearse phone interviews like my life depended on it, because in many ways, it did.

Meanwhile, she'd walk past me without a glance, her eyes glued to her phone, fingers tapping endlessly. I used to be her favorite good morning. Now, I was just an inconvenience in her path.

At first, I tried to talk. I asked her how she was feeling and if she was okay; if we were okay.

Her responses were brief, sharp, and cold.

"I'm fine."

"I don't want to talk about this right now."

"I'm tired."

But what she really meant was, *I'm done.*

I knew it in my gut. That sixth sense, the one you try to ignore when you're hoping to be wrong, screamed louder every day. But I refused to give up on her, on us. I cooked dinner, I cleaned the apartment, and I did everything to show her I was still the man she married.

But no act of love can melt a heart that's already frozen.

Our bedroom became divided by invisible walls; she slept with her back to me every night. Her phone was tucked beneath her pillow like a secret. And me? I lay there staring at the ceiling, heart racing, mind spinning, wondering how the woman I once shared dreams with could become a stranger so quickly.

The silence wasn't peaceful; it was a war, a slow, emotional death. It echoed in every room, filled every meal, haunted every quiet evening.

It was louder than any argument we could've had.

And I began to realize something that shook me to my core:

She was waiting for me to break, so she could justify leaving.

That realization nearly shattered me, but I held on. I smiled through the silence. I made small talk, but she never answered. I kissed her forehead goodnight and whispered, "I love you," knowing I'd receive no reply.

Because sometimes, when you love someone deeply, you accept breadcrumbs and call them a feast.

But let me tell you something:

The most dangerous prison is the one you don't realize you're in, until it's too late.

And I was in one.

A prison built with guilt, self-blame, shame, and emotional manipulation. I began questioning my worth, not because I had failed, but because she no longer saw value in me. When the person you love no longer believes in you, it's easy to lose faith in yourself.

But here's the truth I would later discover: **your value is not tied to someone's ability to recognize it.**

I was still worthy. Still gifted. Still filled with untapped greatness.

But I couldn't see it yet. Not through the fog of rejection. Not through the weight of silence. Not through the nights I sat alone in the living room to avoid the coldness of the bedroom we once called our sanctuary.

She was gone, not physically, not yet. But her soul had already exited the relationship.

And in that emptiness, I had a choice:

- ☒ To sink into the silence with her.
- ☒ Or to start listening to the louder voice within me, the one whispering, *There is more to your life than this.*

But before that choice could fully rise… the worst was yet to come.

Because silence, as painful as it was, would soon be replaced by **the truth**, and **the betrayal** I never saw coming.

But even in the coldest silence, a fire began to flicker inside me. A small one, weak, fragile, but it was there.

And it whispered:

"This is not how your story ends."

Chapter 4:
Betrayal in Broad Daylight

Betrayal doesn't always come with shouting. Sometimes, it arrives quietly with a kiss on the cheek and a lie wrapped in a smile.

I wish I could say I was blindsided. But the truth? I saw it coming, I didn't want to believe it. I wasn't ready to admit that the woman I had once trusted with my life was slowly erasing me from hers.

The signs were there, clear as daylight.

Late-night texts she wouldn't explain. Sudden work events that didn't match her calendar. The mysterious number kept calling and hanging up when I answered. New clothes. Fresh perfume. A glow that had nothing to do with me.

Still, I gave her the benefit of the doubt. Because when you love someone, you try to protect their name, even when they're out there staining yours.

But what's hidden in darkness always comes to light.

One night, I couldn't sleep. I sat on the couch staring at the blank television screen, wondering where I had gone wrong. That's when her phone lit up on the kitchen counter. A name I didn't recognize. A message that shattered me.

"I miss your lips. Can't stop thinking about last night."

My stomach turned. My hands trembled. My mind went numb.

I wanted to believe it was a mistake. Maybe it was someone else's phone, but it wasn't. It was hers and it was real; it was undeniable.

I didn't confront her that night, I just couldn't. I needed time, but I also needed answers. I needed to make sure I wasn't losing my mind.

So, I waited.

Over the next week, I began paying attention, watching, and listening to her routines, stories, and excuses. But I played along, as if everything was fine, because I needed the whole truth before I made a move.

Then one afternoon, while she was out, I checked our shared laptop. I never believed in invading privacy. But betrayal changes your boundaries.

There it was, emails, hidden messages, photos. I saw her secret life, a parallel relationship. While I was breaking under the weight of job loss and trying to keep us together, she was building a life with someone else behind my back.

She wasn't just gone emotionally; she was already gone physically.

The knife wasn't just in my back; it was twisted.

Yet, the deepest pain wasn't just the betrayal; it was the fact that I still loved her.

You don't stop loving someone overnight. You don't switch off the memories, the laughter, the years you've shared. You carry them like ghosts, beautiful and haunting all at once.

But that day, something broke inside me.

Not my heart, that had already been breaking.

What broke was my illusion. My fantasy. My denial. I had to admit to myself, finally:

She was never going to be who I needed.

That truth hurt more than anything. But it also set something else in motion.

I realized I had spent months, maybe years, trying to win over someone who had already left me emotionally. I was auditioning for a love that had long expired. And in that desperation, I had abandoned myself.

But no more.

That day, I made a decision: **I would no longer chase someone who didn't see my worth.** I would stop trying to fix what she had already thrown away.

And as painful as it was, I started the process of reclaiming myself, piece by broken piece.

It wasn't about revenge. It wasn't about anger.

It was about rebirth.

Yes, she betrayed me. Yes, she broke my trust and walked away.

But she did something else too, something she didn't mean to do.

She woke me up.

She forced me to look in the mirror and see a man who had been giving everything to someone who gave nothing in return. She forced me to confront the reality that my value does not decrease because someone failed to see it.

And most of all, she forced me to rise.

Because **when betrayal breaks you, it also builds you, if you let it.**

That chapter closed with tears and pain, yes. But also, with a spark. A decision.

I was no longer the victim in this story.

I was becoming the architect of my comeback.

Chapter 5:
The House I Didn't Know I Bought

Sometimes, betrayal isn't just emotional, it's legal.

Yet, it hits you when you least expect it, in the form of a letter stamped with official seals, sitting coldly on your kitchen table.

I was already drowning in a sea of loss. I was jobless, heartbroken, and alone. The walls of my small apartment felt like they were closing in. I thought I was battling my demons alone, fighting to survive one day at a time.

Then, out of nowhere, this bombshell landed.

A letter from the bank, it was a mortgage statement.

For a house I had never seen, never signed for, never even heard of.

At first, I thought it was a mistake. Maybe a clerical error. Maybe identity theft, yes. But who would do this? And why?

Then the truth hit me like a thunderclap: **She had bought a house in my name without telling me.**

Every word in that letter was a betrayal wrapped in legalese. She had used my name, my credit, my trust, and my identity to secure a mortgage for a home she planned to call her own.

I was left with nothing, not just emotionally, but financially too. The weight of that mortgage was now mine to bear.

I remember sitting at the kitchen table, holding the letter with trembling hands, tears blurring my vision. The world I thought I knew crumbled beneath me. I wasn't just losing my marriage; I was losing my stability, my credit, my future.

In that moment, I could have let the despair swallow me whole and become a victim of her deceit. Instead, I felt something else.

A flicker, a pulse, and a small fierce heartbeat of defiance, because this was more than just about a house; it was a wake-up call. A reminder that I could no longer rely on anyone but myself.

The betrayal was deep, perhaps more profound than the silence we had endured, but it was also a turning point.

I realized I was standing at a crossroads:

I could collapse under the weight of everything she had taken or I could rise, rebuild, and reclaim my life on my own terms.

The choice did not come easily as the path in front of me wasn't clear, but I knew one thing: the resolve was there, and I just had to figure it out.

That night, I sat down and wrote myself a letter.

Not one of bitterness or anger, but one of promise:

"I may have lost my job. I may have lost my marriage. I may have been betrayed by the one I loved most. But I have not lost myself. And I will build a life that no one can take away."

This was the moment my true journey began.

When I realized that being left with nothing was actually the greatest gift I could have received.

Because it forced me to start over.

From scratch, with no crutches, or with no illusions.

I will admit that it was terrifying, but it was also liberating.

That house, which I didn't know I had bought, became the symbol of my past. A past I had to leave behind to move forward.

And in its place, I started to build something new:

A life forged in truth, fueled by grit, and a life that my own success will define.

This chapter wasn't just about betrayal or loss; It was about awakening.

It was about strength.

About the power of starting again, even when the odds seem stacked against you.

I was left with nothing, but I knew that it was only the beginning.

Chapter 6:
Alone in the Dark

After the storm of betrayal, the weight of loss, and the crushing realization of the mortgage deception, I found myself completely alone; physically, emotionally, and spiritually.

I had no job, no wife, no safety net, and no home of my own.

All I had was just a small, dimly lit apartment that suddenly felt like a prison, and the silence was deafening.

I sat on the floor, back against the cold wall, knees pulled close to my chest. The darkness wasn't just around me; it was inside me.

It was heavy.

It was cold.

It was suffocating.

In that darkness, the loudest noise was the one inside my head, the relentless questioning:

"How did I get here?"

"Why did this happen to me?"

"What's the point of fighting if I keep losing?"

It was the darkest night of my life.

I thought about giving up and disappearing into the shadows and never looking back.

As I contemplated the most significant yet heartbreaking decision of my life, something else happened.

I heard a stubborn voice whisper from deep inside me, a voice I hadn't heard in a long time.

"You're still here."

Those three words changed everything.

Being here, broken, bruised, and beaten meant I still had a chance.

I might have lost everything external, but I hadn't lost myself.

I still had breath in my lungs, blood in my veins, fire in my heart, and as long as I had those things, I had hope.

Hope isn't some magical cure; it's not a feeling you wait for to arrive. Instead, it's a decision you make, to keep going, no matter how dark it gets.

I decided, right there on that cold floor, that I would not let this darkness define me.

I would not let this loneliness consume me.

I will fight, survive, and rise.

The next morning, I forced myself out of bed. The weight of despair was still there, but I took a step.

Then another, and another. It was slow and painful, but it was progress.

I reached out to old friends. I asked for help, something I had never done before. In that moment, my pride was replaced by humility.

I started applying for any job I could find, regardless of its size or nature. I took what came, even if it wasn't the career I once dreamed of.

I learned to accept my new reality while refusing to be imprisoned by it.

Then, slowly and piece by piece, the darkness began to lift. Because even in the darkest night, the smallest light can guide you home.

I was alone in the dark, but I was not lost.

I was beginning to find my way back to the man I was meant to be.

Chapter 7:
The Rock Bottom Reality

Hitting rock bottom isn't a moment; it's a slow, grinding process. It's the accumulation of missed calls, unopened letters, empty fridge shelves, and days that bleed into each other with nothing but silence and despair.

For me, rock bottom wasn't a single event. It was living in that small, bare apartment on a mattress on the floor, watching the ceiling for hours, wondering how a man who once had everything could be left with so little.

It was borrowing money for meals, eating sandwiches I barely tasted because hunger had dulled my senses. It was countless job applications met with rejection or, worse, no response at all. I was invisible.

I remember those nights vividly, lying awake and staring into the darkness, feeling the weight of failure crush every hope. The loneliness was brutal, and the shame was unbearable. The dreams I once had felt like distant memories, mocking me from a place I could no longer reach.

But rock bottom, I learned, is paradoxical. It's the lowest point, yes, but it's also a foundation.

When you've lost everything, the only way left is up.

And it was on that floor, surrounded by the debris of a broken life, that I decided I no longer wanted to be there, and there was no way I would let this be the end of my story.

This wasn't just about survival anymore. It was about reclaiming my identity, my dignity, my future.

Therefore, I began the hard work of rebuilding, not with grand gestures or miraculous breakthroughs, but with small, consistent actions:

- ➤ Waking up early, even when my body begged me to stay in bed.
- ➤ Taking the bus to interviews, walking miles to save money.
- ➤ Saying 'yes' to every odd job, no matter how humbling.
- ➤ Learning skills from free online courses.
- ➤ Reaching out to people with honesty and vulnerability.

Each small victory, each step forward, chipped away at the mountain of despair.

Every brick that I laid, I grew stronger, determined, and hopeful.

Rock bottom had forced me to strip away all the pretenses, the pride, the fear, the excuses.

I was raw and honest, and this time I was ready.

This was the crucible where the old me died, and the new me was born, a man forged by fire, hardened by struggle, and fueled by an unbreakable will to rise.

Rock bottom wasn't the end.

It was the beginning of everything.

Chapter 8:
Tears, Regrets, and Rage

There's a brutal honesty in breaking down. A raw, unfiltered release that cleanses the soul but leaves you feeling exposed and vulnerable.

In those early days after losing everything, I cried like I never had before.

Not just tears of sadness, but tears of regret for what was lost, what could have been, and what I had failed to protect.

I regretted trusting too easily, loving too deeply, and giving my all without expecting less in return. I regretted the nights spent hoping for change, the mornings waking up to silence, and the years invested in a future that had vanished overnight.

The tears were a river, flowing from a place of pain too heavy to hold inside.

But tears alone weren't enough, I also felt rage, a fierce, burning fire inside me.

I was furious at the betrayal, injustice, and at myself for not seeing the signs sooner.

That rage could have consumed me. It could have turned me bitter, angry, and broken beyond repair.

But instead, I made a choice.

I decided to channel that rageful emotion to fuel my fight.

I allowed myself to feel every emotion completely, but I refused to be defined by them.

I screamed into pillows, punched walls in empty rooms, and wrote down every painful thought in journals no one would ever read.

I knew that acknowledging my pain was the first step toward healing.

I also realized something profound: pain is inevitable, but suffering is optional.

I could either let this pain destroy me or use it as a catalyst to build something better.

So, with tears on my cheeks and fire in my heart, I vowed to rise.

I embraced my scars as proof of survival; reminders that I had been through hell and was still standing.

This chapter of tears, regrets, and rage was not my defeat.

It was my transformation.

Because sometimes, the darkest emotions birth the strongest warriors.

And I was ready to fight for the life I deserved.

Chapter 9:
The Decision to Fight

There comes a moment in every story of struggle where you stand at a crossroads, one path leading to surrender, the other to battle. I reached that moment in front of the mirror one morning, when my reflection was a stranger's face, tired and worn, but still there.

I looked into my own eyes and asked myself the most challenging question:

"Are you going to give up, or are you going to fight?"

It wasn't a question born from hope or motivation; it came from raw necessity. Because I knew that if I didn't make a choice right then, I would sink further into the abyss.

So I made a promise to myself, to no one else, that I would fight. Not because the battle was easy or the path clear, but because quitting was no longer an option.

That decision was the turning point.

From that day forward, everything changed. My mindset shifted from one of victimhood to that of a warrior. From despair to determination.

I began to see my failures not as dead ends, but as lessons. Every rejection, every setback, became fuel for my fire.

I realized that success wasn't going to find me waiting. I had to go out and claim it, step by step and day by day.

I started with what I had a mind hungry to learn, a body willing to work, and a heart ready to endure.

I devoured books on business, personal development, and resilience. I listened to podcasts by people who had walked through their own fires and come out stronger. I reached out to mentors, to communities, to anyone who could offer guidance or inspiration.

I wrote down my goals, my dreams, and my plan, no matter how small or distant they seemed.

Most importantly, I began to show up. Even on days when every fiber of my being begged me to stay down. Even when the past haunted me and the future felt uncertain.

Because fighting isn't about grand gestures or instant victories, it's about consistency, courage, and commitment.

That decision to fight became my armor against doubt and fear.

It was the silent whisper in the middle of the night that said, **"Keep going."**

The steady heartbeat reminds me, **"You are stronger than you think."**

The unwavering voice that refused to let me settle for less.

From that moment on, I wasn't just surviving. I was preparing to thrive.

And the war for my life had officially begun.

Chapter 10:
Learning to Breathe Again

After making the decision to fight, I quickly realized that strength isn't built overnight. It begins in the small, often unnoticed moments, learning to breathe deeply through the chaos, to find calm amid the storm.

My life had been a whirlwind of pain and uncertainty. So, the first challenge was simple, but profound: **I had to learn how to just breathe again.**

Each morning, I forced myself out of bed, no matter how heavy the weight on my chest. I started taking walks, short, slow walks at first, just to feel the fresh air and remind myself there was still a world beyond my pain.

With every step, I felt a little more alive, and a little less trapped.

I listened to podcasts and audiobooks, soaking up stories of resilience and transformation. These voices became my companions in the early dawn hours, reminders that I wasn't alone and that others had risen from worse.

I practiced mindfulness, focusing on the present moment rather than dwelling on regret or fear. It wasn't easy, and the shadows of my past often crept back in, but with patience and persistence, I found peace in the simple act of breathing.

This process taught me a crucial lesson: **you cannot pour from an empty cup.**

Before I could rebuild my life, I had to rebuild myself.

I began setting small daily goals, drinking water, eating better, stretching, and getting enough sleep. It was a radical act of self-love in a time when I felt unlovable.

I realized that healing is not linear. Some days, I took two steps forward; other days, one step back. But I kept moving, and with every breath, every step, every moment of self-care, I was rediscovering the man I had lost.

Learning to breathe again wasn't just about survival; it was about reclaiming my life, one breath at a time.

Because before you can run, you must learn to stand.

Before you can soar, you must learn to breathe.

And in that breath, I found my first true taste of freedom.

Chapter 11:
The Hustler's Mindset

With my breath steadied and my spirit rekindled, I knew it was time to move beyond mere survival, and it was time to grind to hustle with everything I had left.

But hustle isn't just about working hard. It's about working smart, staying hungry, and embracing every challenge as an opportunity.

I took any job I could find. I worked as a cleaner in offices, delivered packages, and freelanced online. Pride took a backseat, and humility became my closest ally.

Every task, no matter how small or menial, was a building block toward rebuilding my future.

The hustler's mindset is a paradox: it demands patience and persistence, but also relentless urgency. It means understanding that there's no shortcut to success, only a steady, determined march forward.

I woke up early, sometimes before the sun rose, and often worked late into the night. Exhaustion was a constant companion, but I welcomed it.

I made exhaustion my best friend, as it was proof I was moving forward.

Along the way, I learned the importance of adaptability. When one path closed, I found another. When a client said no, I learned from it and improved my pitch. When I felt like quitting, I reminded myself why I started.

This mindset shaped my days; it became the engine behind my transformation.

More than anything, the hustler's mindset taught me resilience. It showed me that setbacks aren't failures, they're just part of the journey.

If I wanted to build everything from nothing, I had to embrace the grind.

Thus, I hustled; relentlessly, fearlessly, and with a heart full of hope and hands ready to work.

Because success doesn't come to those who wait, but it comes to those who refuse to give up.

Chapter 12:
From Couch to Purpose

After months of hustling in jobs that barely paid the bills, I realized something critical: survival wasn't enough anymore. I needed more than just a paycheck; I needed a sense of **purpose**.

For a long time, I had been drifting, working just to get by. But now, the fire inside me demanded something bigger, a vision that could fuel my soul, not just my wallet.

One day, sitting on that worn-out couch in my tiny apartment, I made a decision that would change everything: I would invest in myself. I used the last $100 I had saved to enroll in an online digital marketing course.

It wasn't a luxury, it was a lifeline.

I spent nights hunched over my laptop, learning skills I never thought I could master. SEO, social media strategy, and content creation, terms that had once sounded like foreign languages, became tools I wielded with growing confidence.

Slowly, I began offering my services to small businesses, assisting them in building websites, managing their social media, and growing their brands online.

At first, clients were few and far between. But every website I built, every campaign I crafted, was a step toward something greater.

With each project, I felt a deep sense of pride. This wasn't just work; this was a purpose that I needed, and it gave meaning to my struggle.

That couch was where I had spent most of my days just staring at the ceiling, which once a symbol of stagnation, became the launching pad for my new life.

My toughest days made me realize that no matter where you start, what matters is where you're going.

From the ashes of my broken past, I was forging a future filled with possibility.

Purpose became my compass, and it guided me through the darkest nights and the toughest days, and with purpose lighting the way, I knew I could build everything I had lost, and so much more.

Chapter 13:
Turning Pain into Power

Pain is a powerful teacher. It strips away illusions and forces us to face our deepest truths. But pain doesn't have to be the end, and it can be the beginning of something greater.

As I developed my new skills and began helping others, I grasped something remarkable: my pain was not just a burden to bear, but a source of strength.

Every heartbreak, every betrayal, every moment of despair became fuel for my transformation.

I began to see my story not as a tragedy, but as a testament to resilience.

Instead of hiding my scars, I embraced them. I shared my journey openly, through conversations, blogs, and eventually mentoring others who were facing their own struggles.

Turning pain into power meant taking ownership of my narrative. It meant refusing to be defined by what had been done to me, and instead choosing to define who I wanted to become.

I discovered that when we share our struggles, we create connection and build a bond that reminds us we are not alone.

That vulnerability became a source of healing for me and for others.

I learned to channel my pain into passion; a passion to help, uplift, and inspire, and in doing so, I found a new purpose, one far greater than I had ever imagined.

The pain that once threatened to destroy me had become my greatest source of power.

Because strength isn't about never falling.

It's about rising every time you fall, stronger, wiser, and more determined.

This time, I was determined to rise and turn my weakness into the biggest source of my strength.

Chapter 14:
When Doors Don't Open, Build a Wall

The path to success is rarely smooth, and it is often littered with closed doors, locked gates, and endless waiting. I made sure to learn that waiting for opportunity to knock was a luxury I could no longer afford.

For months, I knocked on countless doors, job applications, client pitches, and networking emails, only to be met with silence, rejection, or polite "no." Every closed door echoed the same message: *not now, not you.*

At first, I felt the sting deeply. Then frustration gnawed at me, whispering doubts in the quiet moments.

I started asking myself, was I good enough? Was I capable? Was my dream just that, a dream?

But in that struggle, a fire was ignited inside me, a refusal to be denied.

If the doors won't open, I decided, I will build my own wall.

A wall so strong, so high, that it becomes a fortress, a place where I control what comes in and goes out.

I didn't have investors, fancy offices, or a network of connections. What I had was determination, grit, and a relentless belief in my potential.

From my small apartment, I launched my own consulting agency. No clients at first. No fancy website, no marketing budget, just a name, a laptop, and a will to succeed.

I cold-called businesses, sent personalized emails, and attended local events. I knocked on a thousand doors until one finally cracked open.

The first client was a small business owner struggling to survive in a crowded market. I worked tirelessly, applying everything I had learned to help them grow. When their sales doubled, word started to spread.

Suddenly, my wall became a gateway. Instead of waiting for permission, I created my own opportunity.

Building that wall was more than just creating a business. It was about reclaiming control over my future, my worth, and my destiny.

I realized that success doesn't wait for you to be ready. It rewards those who are willing to build, to fight, and to persist even when the world says no.

This chapter taught me a powerful lesson:

If life won't open a door for you, don't wait. Build your own wall. And from that wall, build everything.

Because sometimes, the greatest breakthroughs come not from finding a way in, but from creating your own path forward.

Chapter 15:
The Breakthrough Seed

There's a moment every dreamer hopes for, not when success fully arrives, but when it finally shows a flicker of life. For me, that moment came in the form of a single client who said, "Yes."

After endless rejections and ignored proposals, one small business took a chance on me. They didn't have much money, and honestly, neither did I, but what we both had was desperation and a desire for change.

I poured myself into their project as if it were a million-dollar deal. I studied their industry, rebranded their image, rewrote their messaging, and revamped their digital presence from the ground up.

Every night, I stayed up fine-tuning their content, adjusting ads, tracking results, not because they asked me to, but because I had something to prove, not to the world, not even to them, but to **myself**.

Within three months, their online sales more than doubled.

The client was stunned. They called me "a blessing." They told everyone they knew about me. And just like that, the breakthrough seed had been planted.

That one seed didn't just blossom into results; it produced **momentum**.

Soon, referrals started trickling in. I connected with a bakery, then a clothing brand, and then a fitness coach. What started as a hustle from my couch was slowly becoming a stream of business.

But make no mistake, it wasn't magic. It was **faith combined with relentless hard work**.

The breakthrough didn't come with a spotlight. It didn't come with applause. It came quietly, wrapped in sweat, sacrifice, and silent nights of believing when no one else did.

I realized that every bit of pain, every rejection, every sleepless night had prepared me for this moment.

Because the thing about seeds is, they don't grow overnight.

They're buried in dirt, hidden from sight, and tested by time.

But if you keep watering them, with faith, discipline, and resilience, eventually, they break through the soil.

That's what this client represented: proof that the seed I had planted in faith was alive.

And from that one breakthrough, I began to build something sustainable, something scalable, something real.

I wasn't rich yet, nor was I famous, but I was **free**. Free to chase purpose, to create value, and to see results from my relentless effort, finally.

So, if you're in the dark right now, if you're doing the work but seeing no fruit, don't give up.

Your seed is planted.

Your breakthrough is coming.

And when it sprouts, it will change everything.

Chapter 16:
Little Wins, Big Faith

It's easy to celebrate when you land the big deal, win the major contract, or hit your first six figures. But what they don't always tell you is this: greatness is built on **little wins**. Small victories. Quiet milestones. Moments no one else sees.

I remember my first $100 from a paying client. It wasn't much, not compared to what I used to earn in my corporate days, but it felt like a million dollars. Because that $100 meant someone believed in what I had to offer. It meant I was capable, and it meant I was becoming.

After that, it was $250. Then $500. Then $1,000. Not overnight. Not easily. But steadily.

Each time a client said, "Great work," or, "You've helped my business grow," I made it a habit to pause, to breathe, to say thank You to God, and to acknowledge how far I had come.

The world celebrates loud success, but I had learned to find strength in the quiet wins.

I celebrated the nights I stayed up learning new tools.

I celebrated the moments I was afraid to pitch, and did it anyway.

I celebrated not just income, but **impact**, knowing I was helping people succeed, one business at a time.

Faith was my fuel. Not faith in outcomes, but faith in the **process**.

You see, it's not just about believing that something big will happen. It's about believing that your small, consistent efforts matter. That each drop fills the bucket. That each seed leads to a harvest.

There were still tough days, moments when fear whispered, "What if it all falls apart again?"

But I had learned to answer fear with faith: "Even if it does, I'll rebuild again, because I've done it once, and I'm not the same man I was before."

I didn't measure success by zeros in my account, I measured it by how many times I refused to quit, and that was something that kept me going on even on my worst days.

Every email I sent, every job I finished, every person I served, it all added up not just to business growth, but to **internal growth**.

You must understand: greatness doesn't arrive; instead, it accumulates.

It builds, slowly and silently, behind the scenes. While others sleep, you're grinding. While others quit, you're showing up. While others mock the size of your dream, you're quietly building it brick by brick.

That's where real transformation happens, in the repetition, in the resolve, and in the decision to **believe before the breakthrough**.

My little wins built my confidence. My confidence built my consistency. My consistency built my character. And my character built my future.

So, if you're in a season of small wins, don't overlook them.

Celebrate them.

Honor them.

Because little wins, backed by big faith, are the blueprint for a life of unshakable success.

Chapter 17:
The Power of Consistency

Success doesn't show up in an explosion. It doesn't announce itself with fireworks or fanfare. It doesn't knock on your door and say, "Today is the day."

Success is quiet. Slow. Unassuming. It comes disguised as discipline. It comes through **consistency**.

The truth is, talent will only take you so far. Motivation will fade. Excitement comes and goes. But consistency, showing up day in, day out, rain or shine, that is the true engine behind transformation.

After the initial breakthroughs in my business, I found myself standing at a new threshold, not of survival, but of **sustainability**. In order to get there, I had to become obsessed with consistency.

Every morning, I woke up with a plan, even when I didn't feel like it.

I replied to emails even when no one was hiring.

I posted content even when it got zero likes.

I pitched clients even when I feared rejection.

I improved my skills even when I was already good enough.

Because I wasn't chasing perfection, I was chasing **progress**.

I kept a small journal on my desk, nothing fancy, just a worn notebook where I wrote down my daily goals and my daily wins. Some days, the goals were massive. Other days, it was as simple as "Read 10 pages" or "Follow up with 3 prospects." But no matter what, I showed up.

You see, the difference between the successful and the struggling is rarely intelligence or luck; it's **commitment**.

Consistency built my reputation. Clients didn't just come to me for what I offered; they came because they could count on me. They knew

I wouldn't disappear when the project got tough. They knew I delivered, always.

There were no shortcuts, no hacks; just steady steps and a man committed to rising, no matter how long it took.

Consistency made something click in me, and my clarity of vision increased.

Clarity about who I was.

Clarity about what I offered.

Clarity about the future I was building.

And with clarity came confidence. With confidence came momentum, and with momentum came results.

It didn't matter that I didn't have the biggest brand. I had something far more valuable: **trust**, and trust is the currency of success.

But make no mistake, it wasn't always easy. There were days I felt tired, discouraged, and tempted to slow down or give up. Days I wondered if the sacrifices were worth it. But I reminded myself, this wasn't just about income. It was about **impact**. It was about the man I was becoming.

Consistency taught me that mastery isn't a result; it's a lifestyle. You don't become excellent once and for all. You choose excellence **daily**.

And when you do that, the world begins to shift, people start to notice, and opportunities start to appear.

Doors you didn't even knock on begin to open, not because of luck, but because your name now carries weight.

I wasn't waiting for a miracle anymore because I had become the miracle by showing up for myself.

So, if you're reading this, wondering how to climb your own mountain, I'll tell you: **one step at a time**. One post, one call, one hour of focus. And then again tomorrow. And the day after that. And again.

Because the power of consistency is that it compounds.

A single drop of water may seem weak, but with enough time, it carves through stone.

So keep dripping. Keep showing up. Keep going.

The man I am today was not built in a moment of passion, but in **thousands of quiet moments of perseverance.**

Let the world sleep on you if they must.

You just keep building.

Chapter 18:
A New Man Is Born

There comes a time in every comeback story when you look in the mirror, not with shame, regret, or self-pity, but with **pride**.

You recognize the man staring back at you not as the broken shell you once were, but as someone who has been **forged in fire**. And in that moment, you don't just see yourself…

You **meet** yourself.

I remember that morning vividly. The sunlight filtered gently through my blinds as I sat in front of the mirror, fresh from a cold shower, no suit, and no fancy cologne, just me.

And for the first time in years, I didn't flinch. I didn't avoid my own eyes. I looked at myself fully and I smiled.

Because I **knew** the man I had become.

I was no longer defined by loss, betrayal, or the woman who walked away.

I was no longer haunted by the pink slip from the job that let me go.

I was no longer the victim of the sleepless nights, empty bank account, or the silence of loneliness.

I was something else now, something **reborn**.

I had grown calluses on my soul, not from being hard-hearted, but from hard work.

My muscles were no longer just physical; they were mental, emotional, and spiritual.

I had learned to walk alone, speak up, and lead myself when no one else would.

The world hadn't changed. **I had.**

I no longer needed validation. I gave that to myself.

I no longer begged for support. I **became** my own support system.

I no longer feared starting over. I had learned that starting over isn't a weakness, it's wisdom.

I had learned how to be **still**.

How to be **disciplined**.

How to **listen** to the voice within me, not the noise around me.

Every struggle had shaped me, every failure had taught me, and every tear had baptized me into a new season.

You see, we often think rock bottom is a grave, but for me, it was a **garden**.

From that soil of sorrow grew my strength.

From the drought of abandonment came my desire to never leave myself again.

And from the ashes of betrayal, I built belief, not in others, but in **me**.

This new version of me didn't chase people; instead, he chased purpose.

He didn't measure his worth by someone else's love; he became **his own foundation**.

He stopped comparing, stopped competing, and started **creating**.

I had become a man of **substance**, not show.

A man of **principle**. Not pretense.

A man who knew who he was and didn't need to explain it to anyone.

And that's what true success is: becoming someone you can be proud of in the quiet.

Not when the cameras are rolling, or not when the crowd is cheering. But when you're alone with your thoughts, and you feel **peace**.

I forgave myself. I forgave her.

Not because they deserved it, but because I deserved **freedom**.

And you can't carry the weight of greatness while dragging the baggage of bitterness.

So, I cut the rope.

I let go of the past, the pain, the version of me that needed people who didn't choose him.

I buried the boy who needed permission to be enough.

And in his place, **a man was born**.

A man with a mission.

A man who could build an empire not just with his hands, but with his heart.

A man whose identity wasn't tied to what he lost, but to what he **found** in himself.

You may think you need a perfect plan. You don't.

You need a decision: **to become the person your pain was preparing you to be.**

Today, I don't walk with arrogance. I walk with assurance. Not because life is easy, but because I am **equipped**.

And I want you to know this: If you're in the fire, don't fear it.

That fire isn't destroying you, it's **refining** you.

When the dust settles and the wounds heal, you'll rise too.

And when you do, you won't just be healed, you'll be **reborn**.

Chapter 19:
Facing Her Again

Years had passed.

Time is a mysterious healer and revealer, and it has done its work on me. It has changed me and not just my bank account. It not only changed the house I live in now, the suits I wear, or the cars I drive, but also the man I have become.

Success had found me not because I was seeking revenge, but because I was seeking **restoration**. I had rebuilt my life brick by brick, breath by breath, moment by moment, with no one watching, no one clapping, and no one believing in me but me.

And then one day… she showed up.

It was an ordinary afternoon. I had just come out of a business meeting, energized by a new contract that would take my agency to a whole new level. I stopped at a quiet coffee shop, the kind I used to dream about visiting when I was broke and jobless.

As I took a sip of coffee, deep in thought, I looked up and there she was.

Time had changed her, too.

She looked older, not just in appearance but in energy. The sparkle she once carried, the one that had once captivated me, was now a faint flicker behind tired eyes. She smiled, cautiously. I nodded politely. She hesitated, then walked over.

"Can we talk?" she asked quietly, almost apologetically.

I paused.

Not because I still hurt, but because I **didn't**, or not because I was angry, but because I had **nothing left to prove**.

My words refused to come out, so I just nodded, and then we sat down.

She spoke first. "I've followed your journey… I've seen your growth. I'm happy for you."

There was a tremor in her voice. A softness. A weight.

"I didn't know how to face you," she continued. "I was lost back then. I made terrible choices. I was scared, selfish, confused… I don't expect you to forgive me, but I needed to say it out loud."

Her eyes welled with tears, and for a moment, the woman who had once shattered my world was now sitting across from me, not as a villain, not as a monster, but as a human being carrying the **consequences** of her actions.

And here's the truth I never expected to feel: **I didn't hate her.**

Because hate had no room in the house I had built.

I had made peace with the past. I had forgiven her long ago, not for her sake, but for **mine**. I had let go of the bitterness, the betrayal, the sleepless nights. I had stopped asking "Why did she do it?" and started asking, "What did I learn?"

And I had learned everything.

So, I looked at her and said, "I forgive you. I already did."

Her shoulders dropped, as if a mountain she had carried for years had suddenly fallen away.

She looked down, then back up. "You look… happy."

"I am," I said.

I did not say that because I wanted to make her regret, but because I meant it.

I didn't need her approval anymore. I didn't need her apology. But I also didn't need to punish her. Because I had risen. And in rising, I had realized something powerful:

The best closure isn't revenge. It's becoming everything they thought you couldn't be.

We talked for a while longer. She told me about her struggles, how the relationship she left me for had ended badly, and how she lost the house. She had to start over from scratch. I listened without judgment, without pride, without gloating.

Because that's what healed people do.

Before we parted, she said, "I used to think you wouldn't survive without me."

I smiled. "I used to think that too. But losing you was the best thing that ever happened to me."

Not because it was painless, but because it **forced me to grow**.

We stood up and maintained our distance; we gave no hugs, and no tears were shed. It was a simple nod, but I meant something profound. It was a nod that says:

I've moved on, and I wish you well.

And as she walked away, I realized something profound.

The man who had once been broken, abandoned, and defeated was gone.

In his place stood a man of clarity. Of strength. Of vision.

I didn't just survive her betrayal.

I transcended it.

I no longer needed to rewrite the past.

Because the future I had built was far more beautiful.

And sometimes, that's the greatest gift life gives us:

The chance to rise so high that you no longer need to look back.

Chapter 20:
Closure, Not Revenge

There's a temptation in pain and a dangerous allure.

When someone betrays you, hurts you, walks away when you're at your lowest, a voice inside screams: **"You'll see. I'll make you regret this. I'll win, to show you what you lost."**

That's revenge talking and it's seductive.

For a time, it fueled me. I can admit that now. When I was broke, when I was sleeping on the floor, when I was staring at job rejections and eating ramen noodles, I imagined the day I'd see her again, and she'd realize just how badly she messed up. I wanted her to feel what I had felt: abandoned, unseen, discarded.

But something happened on my way to the top...

I healed.

And when you truly heal, revenge no longer satisfies you, because you've gained something far more powerful: **peace**.

Closure doesn't come from proving a point.

It comes from no longer needing to.

I used to think closure was a conversation, an apology, a grand reconciliation where all the wrongs were made right. But now I know, **closure is an inside job**.

It's not something they give you.

It's something you decide for yourself.

I decided to stop checking her social media.

I decided to stop replaying our final arguments in my head.

I decided to stop wondering how she could love someone else while I was falling apart.

And the moment I let those thoughts go, I reclaimed my power.

Revenge wants the world to see you win so that someone else can lose. In contrast, closure wants you to win whether they see it or not.

And here's what I've learned: **Your growth doesn't need an audience.**

There were no cameras when I cried on the bathroom floor.

No applause when I finally landed my first freelance gig.

No headlines when I paid off my debt, one bill at a time.

But those quiet victories? They were mine, and they mattered more than any public success.

Closure came in waves.

It came when I stopped trying to understand her betrayal.

It came when I stopped defining my worth based on her leaving.

It came when I realized that forgiveness wasn't letting her off the hook; it was setting **myself** free.

And the irony? The more I let go, the more I grew.

My business took off.

My influence expanded.

My health improved.

My mindset elevated.

And the peace I found… it was unshakable.

I no longer walked into rooms needing to prove anything.

I no longer sought validation in likes, applause, or someone's opinion of my past.

Because **I knew who I was**, and that was enough.

Revenge is noisy.

Closure is quiet.

Revenge looks outward.

Closure looks inward.

Revenge says, "Look what I did without you."

Closure says, "I became who I was meant to be, because of everything, even the pain."

But having closure does not mean that I forgot the pain I had endured. I still remember the hurt. I remember the night she left, the lies, the silence, the cold. I remember the bank notice about the house she bought behind my back. I remember feeling disposable.

But I remember something else, too.

I remember the night I promised myself I wouldn't stay broken.

I remember the first time I laughed again.

The first time I helped someone else through their storm.

The first time I woke up and didn't feel like a failure.

And I hold those memories tighter.

That's what closure is. It's not forgetting what happened, it's refusing to let it define you.

It's saying: **"I've bled, I've bent, but I did not break. And now, I rise."**

I didn't rise to shame her, make her jealous, or post about it online.

I rose for me.

For the man I promised I'd become.

For the life I deserved.

For the peace I fought for.

And if I could offer you anything, dear reader, it's this:

Don't chase revenge. Chase freedom.

Don't become so obsessed with making them regret that you forget to make yourself proud.

Let your success be sacred.

Let your joy be private.

Let your healing be your revenge.

And when the moment comes, if it ever does, when you look them in the eye again… let it not be from a place of spite, but from a place of **strength**.

Let your silence speak.

Let your composure shine.

Let your peace say everything your pain once screamed.

And walk away, not because you lost anything, but because you finally **won** yourself back.

That's the real victory.

That's closure.

Chapter 21:
Standing on My Own Empire

There's a moment in every redemption story where the dust settles, the wounds have scarred over, and you look around… and realize you made it.

You're no longer crawling. You're no longer scraping for survival. You're standing, tall, steady, strong, in the life you rebuilt with your bare hands.

And that's precisely where I found myself.

After years of pain, betrayal, rebuilding, sacrifice, and relentless effort… I stood at the center of an empire that was once just a **dream in my heart and a plan on a scrap of paper.**

But let me be honest, it didn't feel grand or cinematic.

It felt **earned**.

Not gifted. Not inherited. Not handed to me because of luck.

I earned every inch of this mountain I climbed.

When I launched my consulting agency from my small apartment with no capital, no clients, and only a broken heart pushing me forward, I had no blueprint. Just hunger. Just grit. Just an unshakable refusal to quit.

That first client who took a chance on me? I served them like they were my only ones, because they were, and I made sure to give them **excellence**.

That turned into a referral.

Which turned into a small wave.

Then a flow.

Then a flood.

Before long, I wasn't chasing clients; they were finding me.

Not because I had a fancy office or a big team. But because **I had results**. I had integrity. I had passion that couldn't be faked and a fire that couldn't be extinguished.

Success didn't come overnight.

It came **after the nights I didn't sleep**, staying up to fix broken code, revise marketing decks, and read books on leadership and growth.

It came after the weekends I skipped parties to build landing pages.

It came after months of eating simply, living humbly, and investing every dollar back into my business.

It came after the days I fought self-doubt, battled imposter syndrome, and showed up anyway.

And when it came, when the business scaled, when the revenue multiplied, when my name started to mean something in the industry, I didn't celebrate with ego. I celebrated with **gratitude**.

I remembered what it felt like to have nothing.

I remembered counting coins at the gas station.

I remembered hearing her footsteps as she walked away.

I remembered sleeping on the floor, cold and alone.

And now... here I was. **Not just surviving. Thriving.**

The small apartment? Upgraded to a penthouse with a skyline view.

The one-man hustle? Now a whole team, talented, dedicated, passionate.

The consulting gig? Now a seven-figure agency with clients across countries and industries.

The broken man? Now whole, healed, and **on fire with purpose**.

But what mattered most wasn't the money.

It was **who I became** in the process.

I became a leader, a mentor, and a man who didn't just rebuild a life, **he built a legacy**.

Because what good is success if it only serves you?

I began giving back by creating programs to mentor young entrepreneurs, offering free workshops in underserved communities, and partnering with nonprofits to teach financial literacy and resilience.

I wanted my story to mean something more than just a comeback.

I wanted it to be a **compass** for others, a guide that says, "Yes, you can start over. Yes, you can rise. Yes, you can lose everything and still **build everything**."

And perhaps the most surreal moment of all?

I was invited to speak at a business summit. There were thousands in the audience. I had spotlights, cameras, and media covering my speech.

As I stood on that stage, dressed in a sharp suit, holding a microphone, I thought back to the man who once whispered affirmations to himself to get out of bed. The man who felt invisible. The man who was laughed at, lied to, and left behind.

Now they listened to him, they clapped for him, and were even inspired by him.

That moment didn't inflate my pride; it humbled me to my core.

Because I realized something powerful:

You are never truly defeated unless you quit.

You can be betrayed.

You can lose it all.

You can cry, stumble, fail, and fall a hundred times.

But as long as you keep rising… your story is still being written.

I stood on that stage, not to prove I had made it, but to **show others what's possible**.

To be a living example of resilience.

To say, "If I could do it, so can you."

I wasn't supposed to win.

By every statistic, a broken marriage, financial ruin, and depression, I should have faded into the background, settled for less, and stayed small.

But **I chose more**.

And here I stood, not as a victim of betrayal, but as a **builder of dreams**.

This empire I now lead? It's not made of marble and glass.

It's made of **pain repurposed into power**.

Of **lessons etched in scars**.

Of **faith, even when I had no evidence to believe.**

So, if you're reading this, standing in your own ruins, let this be a prophecy:

You are not done. You are only becoming.

Your past may be shattered, but your future is still whole.

Your pain is not pointless. It's preparing you.

Your storm is not the end; it's the beginning of your building phase.

One day, you'll look back, not with bitterness, but with wonder.

You'll say, "I made it."

And the world won't believe what you built from nothing.

But you'll know.

Because you were there, when the lights were off, when the world walked out, when you had no one but God and grit.

You'll stand on your empire, not built of revenge, but of **rebirth**.

And that… that is the most tremendous success of all.

Chapter 22:
Left with Nothing, Built Everything

There's something sacred about standing at the end of a long road, a road littered with heartbreak, betrayal, tears, and triumph. And looking back, not in regret, but in awe.

I began this journey stripped of everything I thought mattered: my job, my relationship, my home, my dignity. I didn't just hit rock bottom, I *lived* there. I breathed it in. I sat with the pain. I tasted despair in its purest form.

And yet, from those ashes, **I rose**.

My rise wasn't quick nor was it easy, but it was steady.

I rose because something inside me refused to die, that tiny, flickering flame of belief. That whisper that said, *"This can't be the end."* That stubborn piece of me that chose fight over flight, purpose over pity, and destiny over defeat.

I was left with nothing, **but nothing became the raw material for everything**.

When the world stripped me of my status, it gave me authenticity.

When betrayal robbed me of love, it introduced me to self-worth.

When I lost my comfort, I gained my calling.

And when I was alone, I found the most powerful person I'd ever met, **myself.**

You see, success isn't built in the spotlight.

It's forged in silence.

In the dark.

In the quiet moments where no one is clapping.

No one is watching.

And quitting feels easier than continuing.

But those are the *defining* moments.

That's when champions are made, not by what they have, but by what they do when they have **nothing**.

I didn't win because life got easier. I won because I got **stronger**.

I stopped waiting for someone to rescue me and became my own savior.

I stopped begging for doors to open and built my own.

I stopped replaying the betrayal and started rewriting my future.

And now, I live not just with success, but with *peace*.

Not just with money, but with *meaning*.

Not just with influence, but with *impact*.

Because I made a choice long ago:

To stop surviving and start building.

To stop bleeding over my brokenness and start bleeding purpose into my pain.

To stop being the victim and become the *author* of my comeback story.

This book is not just the tale of one man's journey.

It's a mirror.

A reflection of what's possible for *you*.

Because I know what it feels like to be abandoned.

To be overlooked.

To be underestimated.

To scream into the void and hear nothing back.

But I also know what it feels like to make a comeback so powerful that even the past has to respect your future.

You may be standing in ruins right now.

You may be holding the broken pieces of a life you thought would last.

But listen to me, you are not finished.

You are being *forged*.

Every heartbreak is carving out space for strength.

Every failure is fertilizing the soil of your future.

Every tear is watering seeds you haven't even seen bloom yet.

Don't give up. Don't fold. Don't retreat.

You were not created to fail.

You were created to rise, despite your loss, but *because of it*.

Let the betrayal push you.

Let the heartbreak fuel you.

Let the silence sharpen you.

Let the pain teach you.

Let the rock bottom refine you.

And when you rise, not if, but **when**, rise with dignity.

Rise without vengeance.

Rise without ego.

Rise with love, humility, and fire.

Build the kind of life that silences doubt.

That answers every "You can't" with "I did."

That becomes the blueprint for others to follow.

You were left with nothing?

Good.

Now you have the most incredible opportunity of all, to **build everything**.

Not just a business.

Not just wealth.

But **character. Power. Wisdom. Legacy.**

Your story isn't over, it's just beginning.

And one day, someone will read your life the way you're reading mine right now.

And they'll believe again.

Because you proved that a man, betrayed, broken, and buried, can still rise.

Can still reignite.

Can still rebuild.

It can still become **unshakable**.

So, here's to your ashes.

Here's to your beginnings.

Here's to the mountain you're about to climb.

Let this be your declaration:

I was left with nothing. But I built everything.

And I will do it again, if I must, because now I know who I am.

And I know what I'm made of.